(Right)
Delftware basket
English or Continental,
dated 1681

(Front cover)
Earthenware teapot with majolica glazes
English, Minton, Staffordshire, 1874

(Back cover)
Stoneware tabby cat
English, Charles Vyse, 1933

Published for the National Museums & Galleries on Merseyside by:
The Bluecoat Press
Bluecoat Chambers
School Lane
Liverpool L1 3BX

Design by:
March design, Liverpool

ISBN 0 906367 83 2

© The Board of Trustees of the National Museums & Galleries on Merseyside.

All rights reserved. No part of this publication may be reproduced, stored in a retrieval system, or transmitted in any form or by any means, electronic, mechanical, photocopying, recording or otherwise, without prior permission from the publisher.

The Art of the Potter

European Pottery in the National Museums & Galleries on Merseyside

E. Myra Brown

The Middle Ages and the Medieval Tradition

*1 Earthenware watering pot
English, probably London,
16th century*
*2 Saltglazed stoneware bottle
or 'bellarmine'
German, about 1600*
*3 Slipware dish or 'charger'
English, Staffordshire, 1660-80
Probably made by
William Talor*

In medieval Europe, pottery was a humble product, providing the jugs and cooking pots for ordinary people. It was made of a rough earthenware, usually unglazed, and was often fired in makeshift bonfires called 'clamps'. Potters used locally dug clays, found their fuel locally for firing, and served a local market.

By the late 13th century, lead-based glazes and more efficient kilns were in use and a wide range of wheel-thrown pottery and floor tiles were produced. Earthenware (fired to about 1000 degrees Celsius) is easily stained by food and drink unless protected by the glassy surface of a glaze. Glass melts at a high temperature, but this can be lowered by adding other ingredients, such as lead, to the glaze. Lead glazes were often dusted onto the surface of a pot with a rag, giving it a patchy appearance. The 16th-century watering pot (1) was probably glazed in this way. The pot was for everyday use, for damping down the dust on rush-covered floors.

The much stronger stoneware (see p. 12), developed in Germany, was exported all over Europe from the 15th century. This saltglazed stoneware bottle (2) or 'bellarmine' would have been used for containing wine or other liquor. It is relief-decorated with faces including a bearded mask applied to the neck. In England, the Protestants said that this mask represented the Roman Catholic Cardinal Bellarmino. 'Bellarmines' were also later made in England.

Pottery could be coloured using glazes stained with metallic ores such as copper, but to produce patterns in colour the potter used liquid clay, known as slip. A pot of red or buff clay would be dipped in a slip of the rarer white clay. Designs in a different coloured slip were then trailed on with a nozzle – rather like icing a cake. 'Slipware', as this kind of pottery is known, was made in several areas of Britain from the 17th century onwards, notably Staffordshire, Devon and Essex. The large dish (3) or 'charger', slip-trailed with a cavalier and lady, is signed 'WILLIAM TALOR'. This is thought to be the name of the potter who made it rather than the customer who ordered it.

In the 18th century, other types of pottery ousted slipware from the upper end of the pottery market although local potteries continued to produce slipware and simple 'coarse' earthenware well into the 20th century.

3

The Tin-Glaze Tradition – Maiolica, Delft, Faience

Tin-glazed earthenware is covered in a lead glaze which is made opaque and white by the addition of tin oxide. This coating of glaze hides the buff-coloured earthenware body. The technique originated in the Near East in the 9th century and was brought to Spain by the Moors. From Spain, the technique spread to almost all of Europe. Tin-glazing was an important development because, unlike brown lead-glazed earthenwares, the tin-glaze created a white surface which could be painted in bright colours, including a vivid blue.

In Italy the tin-glazed ware was known as 'maiolica', named after the island of Majorca through which the ware was exported from Spain. Maiolica was, in turn, produced in a number of Italian towns – most notably Faenza but also Gubbio, Deruta and Naples. This drug jar (4) is painted in the 'istoriato' or story-telling style with a scene showing Adam and Eve covering themselves before God in the Garden of Eden. It is one of a number of jars with Biblical themes, used to contain dry drugs in a monastic pharmacy.

The French tin-glaze factories of the 16th and early 17th centuries were dominated by the Italian maiolica style – hence the use of the term 'faience' (from Faenza in Italy) to describe the ware. By the 18th century, a more distinctly French style began to emerge. Practical but decorative wares like this water-cistern (5), originally with a matching water-basin, were made alongside the more usual tablewares. The painting on the cistern is typical of the Moustiers factory, with a miniature mythical scene, here depicting Perseus rescuing Andromeda from the sea monster, within a floral border and surrounded by festoons of flowers.

Italian potters also introduced tin-glazing to the Netherlands and, from about 1550, the technique spread further to North Germany (where it was termed 'fayence') and England. In the 18th century it became known as 'delftware' as, by then, the Dutch town of Delft had become one of the major centres for tin-glaze manufacture in Europe.

In England, delftware was mainly made in London, Bristol and, from the early 1700s, Liverpool. At first it was influenced by the Flemish potters and is reminiscent of Italian maiolica. Later, the shapes and decoration of imported Chinese blue and white

4 *Maiolica drug jar or 'albarello'*
Italian, Naples, 1757
Probably painted by Pasquale Criscuola

5 *Faience water-cistern and cover*
French, Olerys-Laugier factory,
Moustiers, about 1740
Painted by Jean-Francois Pelloquin

6 *Delftware ship bowl:*
'Success to ye Prussian Hero'
English, Liverpool, 1769

porcelain were imitated and adapted. This European style is called 'chinoiserie'.

The Liverpool ship bowl (6) combines both European and oriental images. The interior is painted with a portrait of a ship, the *Prussian Hero*; the outside with a chinoiserie scene. These punch bowls were probably made as special commissions for the owner or captain of the named ship and may have been used to toast the vessel on its return from a successful voyage. Maritime records show that the *Prussian Hero* was a 400-ton privateer (that is, a privately armed vessel licensed to attack enemy ships – or 'licensed pirate'), with a crew of 80 under the command of Captain Day and was engaged in the American and West Indies trade. The ship's name refers to Frederick the Great, King of Prussia, an ally of England in the 1760s.

Tin-glazed ware was not especially serviceable as it was easily chipped or cracked and, by the end of the 18th century, it was superseded by other improved types of pottery, in particular creamware.

White Gold

Marco Polo, visiting China in the 13th century, was the first European to describe porcelain and to name it, 'porcellana', after a special kind of shell. Only a trickle of porcelain found its way from China to Europe until the 17th century, when the Dutch and English East India Companies began large-scale trade with China.

Europeans marvelled at the whiteness, hardness, delicacy and translucency of porcelain, but did not know how to make it. As more and more porcelain was exported from the East to satisfy an ever-growing demand, Europeans struggled to find out how it was made. In 1708, Johann Friedrich Böttger, a young alchemist, was engaged by Augustus, Elector of Saxony, to discover the secret of making porcelain. At first he succeeded in making a fine and extremely hard, red stoneware. The small teapot (7) shows how it could be engraved, cut and polished – like semi-precious stone or metal.

Soon after, Böttger successfully created a true white porcelain and, in 1710, the Meissen porcelain factory was founded. The porcelain made in China and at

7 *Red stoneware teapot and cover*
Meissen, Johann Friedrich Böttger, about 1708-19

7

8 Hard-paste porcelain teawares from a travelling breakfast service Meissen porcelain factory, about 1725-30 Possibly painted by Johann Gregorius Höroldt

Meissen was composed of china clay (kaolin) and a related mineral called china stone, fired to a high temperature of about 1400 degrees Celsius. The travelling service (8) was made during the early years of the Meissen factory. Although unsigned, it was possibly painted by Johann Gregorius Höroldt, famed for his use of rich enamel colours. The service would have been stored in a leather-covered wooden box, ready for transporting in a horse-drawn carriage.

Imitation porcelains, composed of different materials and fired at lower temperatures, were made as early as the 16th century. Such imitations are known as 'soft-paste' to distinguish them from the true or 'hard-paste' porcelains. The early British porcelain factories made soft-paste porcelains and produced more tea-ware than dinner-ware, since larger pieces like plates and dishes often warped in the firing. These factories found it difficult to compete with the technically superior Chinese hard-paste porcelain. Customers often preferred to buy the imports because they could be trusted to withstand boiling water. Some English manufacturers advised customers to warm up teapots gradually to prevent them from 'flying' into pieces.

The Chelsea factory, in production by 1745, at first used a glassy body which was beautiful but not strong. However, the factory's fashionable customers were probably more concerned with appearance than durability. The form of this splendid coffee or chocolate pot (9), decorated with flowering branches, was probably derived from a shape originally used for a silver pot.

Soft-paste porcelain and, later, a type of hard-paste porcelain were also made in Liverpool. In all, seven porcelain sites are known to have existed there. The earliest were those of William Reid, Samuel Gilbody and Richard Chaffers, who all started porcelain production around 1755. The works of both Samuel Gilbody and Richard Chaffers were situated on Shaw's Brow, later William Brown Street, where the Liverpool Museum now stands. The Liverpool factories mainly produced table and teawares, although figures and busts were also made. This bust of George II (1683-1760) (10), one of fourteen known to exist, is an unusual attempt to produce portrait sculpture in porcelain.

9 *Soft-paste porcelain chocolate or coffee pot and cover*
English, Chelsea porcelain factory, about 1744-49

10 *Soft-paste porcelain bust of George II*
English, Richard Chaffers' factory, Liverpool, about 1755-60

Fine Stoneware and Dry Bodies

Stoneware is pottery fired to such a high temperature (about 1250 degrees Celsius) that the ingredients fuse together to make a water-tight body of stony hardness. It can be glazed quite simply by throwing a handful of ordinary salt into the kiln when it is at its hottest. In the heat, the sodium in the salt separates out and is deposited over the surface of the pots as a very thin, hard layer. A salt glaze is usually marked by tiny pits over the surface, rather like the texture of orange peel.

European stoneware was first developed in Germany in the 13th to 14th centuries, and the saltglaze technique about a hundred years later. It was especially useful for pots that needed to stand rough usage, like

11

tavern bottles and jugs (see p. 4). At the same time, large amounts were imported into England. Stoneware was also used for more decorative items such as the inkstand (11), modelled with figures and lions, one of which supports a candle or taper-holder.

In 1672, John Dwight of the Fulham Pottery, near London, was granted a patent to manufacture stoneware pots in 'our Kingdom of England where they have not hitherto been wrought or made'. Dwight had ambitions for his stoneware and produced a small number of beautifully modelled figures and busts, mostly in a white or light-coloured clay. Another group, representing classical gods like this figure of Jupiter (12), were made in a light brown to look like bronze. Dwight also made unglazed red stoneware in imitation of that imported from China. The ingredients of this were so finely ground and carefully mixed that a smooth surface could be achieved.

Unglazed red stoneware was made briefly in Staffordshire by the Elers brothers in the 1690s, but other potters in the area do not appear to have made the ware until the 1740s. The coffee pot (13), decorated with chinoiserie reliefs, is an example of Staffordshire red stoneware dating from the 1750s-60s.

11 Grey saltglazed stoneware inkstand Probably German, 18th century

12 Brown saltglazed stoneware figure of Jupiter English, John Dwight's factory, Fulham, about 1675

12

13 Red stoneware coffee pot and cover
English, Staffordshire, 1750-60
14 White saltglazed stoneware tea canister
English, Okill's Flint Mug Works, Liverpool, 1760
Probably made by Henry Muskitt

By 1720, Staffordshire potters were making white saltglazed stoneware, which looked a little like porcelain, using ground flint and special white clays brought from Devon and Dorset. White saltglazed stoneware was also made in Liverpool at Okill's Flint Mug Works, where a potter called Henry Muskitt was apprenticed. Amongst the few identifiable examples by him is this small tea canister (14) with 'scratch blue' or incised decoration. It is inscribed with the name 'Henry Muskit 1760 L' and 'Elizabeth Cannon 1760 Liverp'.

At first, white saltglaze was decorated with moulded or applied reliefs like the red stoneware but, from about 1750, it began to be painted in enamel colours like porcelain. In the 1760s, Josiah Wedgwood's improved cream-coloured earthenware began to win the market from white saltglazed stoneware and it gradually went out of favour.

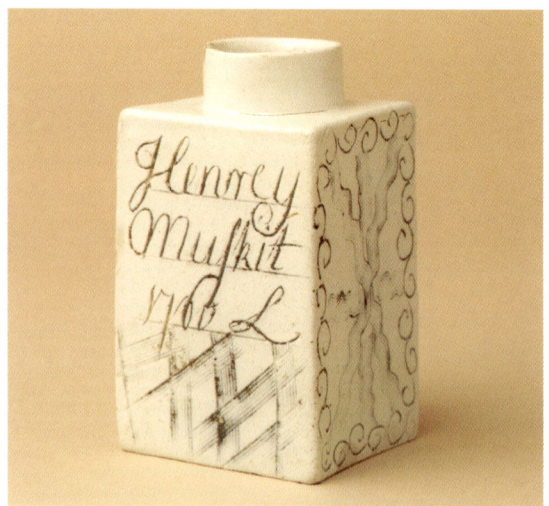

13

14

A New Etruria – The Age of Wedgwood

Josiah Wedgwood (1730-1795) made his fortune by lightening the colour of the lead-glazed earthenware known to his contemporaries simply as 'the cream colour' and to modern collectors as creamware. As shrewd in marketing as in manufacturing, he used royal patronage to rename it 'Queensware'. The lighter colour made it resemble porcelain, as did the printed decoration applied for him from 1761 by John Sadler and Guy Green in Liverpool.

Wedgwood produced creamware for every conceivable commercial, industrial and domestic use. This creamware jelly mould core (15), painted in enamels, was for ornamenting the dessert table. It was used with an outer mould to form a thin coating of jelly. After removing the outer mould, the painted decoration could be seen through the clear jelly.

When the swing of taste to the Neo-classical created a market for pottery in the Greek or Roman style,

15 *'Queensware' or creamware jelly mould core English, Josiah Wedgwood, Staffordshire, about 1790*

16 *Painted black basalt vase English, Josiah Wedgwood, Staffordshire, about 1790*

17 Black jasper 'Portland' vase and base with white reliefs
English, Josiah Wedgwood, Staffordshire, 1792-93
18 Creamware 'Stella' ewer with gilding, on a black basalt base
English, Josiah Wedgwood, Staffordshire, about 1775

Wedgwood saw the potential of dry-bodied stoneware and built a new factory to produce it. At that time the ancient Greek vases being unearthed from tombs in Tuscany were thought to be Etruscan, and Wedgwood therefore called his factory Etruria. It began production in 1769. He aimed his vases and ornaments at the fashion-conscious upper end of the market, a daring thing for pottery to attempt. He succeeded thanks to the Liverpool businessman Thomas Bentley whom he persuaded to go into partnership with him. Bentley's nose for fashionable taste made him the perfect choice to run the London end of the business, dealing with the designers, the firm's showroom, and London society. The ornamental wares were marked 'Wedgwood and Bentley' until Bentley's death in 1780.

The first productions of Etruria were in the black body which Wedgwood named 'basaltes' to suggest ancient sculpture carved from black basalt. Some of

17

these black wares were painted in imitation of Greek vases such as the vase (16), decorated with 'The Race of Atlanta and Hippomenes'.

In about 1775 Wedgwood perfected a body which could be stained in different colours, with a contrasting colour – usually white – for the applied reliefs. Wedgwood named it 'jasper' after the semi-precious stone used for carved cameos. The 'Portland' vase (17) is probably Wedgwood's most famous achievement. It was copied from a carved cameo glass vessel of Roman origin dating from the 1st century B.C., now in the British Museum, and once owned by the Duchess of Portland. At least 35 first-edition 'Portland' vases were made during the lifetime of Josiah Wedgwood I between 1791 and 1796, of which 34 are still known to exist.

Jasper is the product most people still associate with Wedgwood today. He deliberately tried to make his wares resemble the hardstones which were then fashioned into boxes and other small works known as *objets de vertu*. His stated ambition was to make his products 'unpotlike', as can be seen in this 'Stella' ewer (18), derived from a design by the French painter and etcher, Jacques Stella. The stone-like quality was achieved by dusting the surface with metal oxides before glazing.

18

Export through Liverpool

19 *Wood-block printed tile English, Liverpool, printed by John Sadler, 1756-57*
20 *Copper-plate printed tile English, Liverpool, printed by John Sadler, 1758-61*

Liverpool was not only a centre for pottery- and porcelain-making in the 18th century, it was also the main port of export for the growing Staffordshire pottery industry. As the bulk of production was for export, Liverpool's part in this trade was vital. Pottery was at first brought by pack horses to Liverpool but, with the opening of the Trent & Mersey Canal in 1777, business thrived.

In 1756, the Liverpool printer John Sadler and his partner Guy Green developed a technique of printing on tin-glazed tiles. Their sworn affidavit, dated 2 August 1756, stated that within 'six hours they did print upwards of 1200 earthenware tiles'. For a short time, wood-blocks were used for transferring the image, but these were soon superseded by engraved copper-plates. Designs were taken from a variety of sources. The wood-block printed tile in blue (19) shows a lady and gentleman in hunting costume. This design was taken from a series of prints entitled *Caffee, The und Tabac Zieretten* by J.E. Nilson. The other tile (20), printed with a scene depicting *The Sailor's Farewell*, is derived from an engraving by T. Booth after Boitard.

In 1761, Sadler made an agreement with Josiah Wedgwood of Staffordshire to print his creamware. This cream-coloured earthenware became one of Liverpool's most important exports. It was the first type of pottery to look as delicate as porcelain and yet be reasonably strong. The inscribed creamware punch bowl (21), made by Wedgwood and printed in Liverpool, was probably decorated as a commission for a captain in the Baltic trade.

In 1796, the Herculaneum Pottery was founded on

21 *Transfer-printed creamware ship bowl*
English, Josiah Wedgwood, Staffordshire
Printed in Liverpool, 1788

22 Pearlware bust of George Washington
English, Herculaneum Pottery, Liverpool, about 1800

23 Transfer-printed creamware jug
English, Herculaneum Pottery, Liverpool, 1805-06

the banks of the River Mersey in Toxteth, to take advantage of an export boom. At first, it mainly employed Staffordshire workers and the factory produced the full range of Staffordshire-type wares, including porcelain. Special lines were made for the American markets, like this bust of George Washington (22). Other commemoratives were also produced such as the large jug (23) decorated with numerous transfer-prints including those of the British heroes, Earl St Vincent, Lord Duncan and Lord Nelson. The date of Nelson's death in October 1805 is recorded below his portrait. The Herculaneum factory continued to operate until 1840 when local investment shifted away from pottery-making to maritime industries such as ship-building and dock-construction.

Nineteenth-Century Extravagance

The mid-19th century saw the British pottery industry responding to the expanding prosperity created by the Industrial Revolution. Manufacturers sought to meet the needs of both a new, urbanised working class and an affluent middle class. As well as supplying large foreign and colonial markets, British potteries had to face the challenge of imports from fast-developing factories abroad. This competitiveness encouraged technical improvements and stimulated inventiveness. Increasingly, pottery and porcelain was cast in moulds instead of being modelled by hand. In 1844 an unglazed porcelain was developed by Copeland & Garrett which imitated white marble. Named 'Parian', after the famous marble quarried on the Greek island of Paros, it was used by many factories for making figures like the group (24) showing a scene from

24 *Parian figure group*
'Britomartis Unveiling Amoret'
English, Coalport, Shropshire,
about 1851
Modelled by Joseph Pitts

25 *Earthenware teapot with majolica glazes*
English, Minton, Staffordshire, 1874

26 *Jasperware pot-pourri vase and cover*
English, Josiah Wedgwood, Staffordshire, about 1850

Spencer's poem *The Faerie Queene*, as well as for scaled-down replicas of marble statues.

The novel and the varied were in great demand. In 1849, Leon Arnoux developed the 'Majolica' glaze for the firm of Minton in Staffordshire. 'Majolica' was officially introduced at the Great Exhibition of 1851 and, being both bold and colourful, appealed to Victorian taste. The monkey teapot (25), with a removable head as the lid, shows the use of moulded shapes combined with the bright majolica glazes.

The Victorian taste for the eclectic led to all past styles being utilised for inspiration or copying. Where Nature was considered the best model to copy, this frequently meant a literal copying – as can be seen by the applied floral reliefs on the pot-pourri vase made of jasperware (26).

25

26

The Arts and Crafts Movement in Pottery

The ideas and writings of the critic John Ruskin (1819-1900) and the designer William Morris (1834-1896) strongly influenced a number of designers and makers, including potters, from the mid-19th century. They rejected the factory mass-production of the Victorian era in favour of handwork and the importance of the craftsman. This reaction against industrialisation and a return to craft values is known as the Arts and Crafts Movement. The Birkenhead firm, the Della Robbia Pottery Company (1893-1906) was run on Arts and Crafts lines. The workers, including women from the local art schools, were encouraged to develop their own ideas and to sign their work. Useful wares such as vases and bowls were produced as well as a

27 Earthenware tile panels
English, Della Robbia Pottery, Birkenhead, about 1900

27

28 *Earthenware plate*
Decorated by the Minton Art
Pottery Studio, London, 1873
29 *Earthenware flask*
Designed by Christopher Dresser
English, Linthorpe Art Pottery,
Middlesbrough, about 1880-90

28

29

number of architectural commissions. The two tile panels (27), showing scenes from 'The Six Days of Creation' after a design by the artist Edward Burne-Jones, were originally installed in the Mill Street Mission, Toxteth, Liverpool.

The second half of the 19th century also saw a greater emphasis on 'good design', again a reaction to badly-designed factory products. Co-operation between some of the larger pottery manufacturers and local art schools encouraged the setting up of pottery studios such as those at Doulton's in Lambeth and Minton's Art Pottery Studio in Kensington, London. The plate (28) decorated with a medieval scene was painted at the Minton Studio on blanks supplied by the parent company in Staffordshire.

There was a strong interest in the revival of ancient styles, such as Gothic, Persian and Chinese, which were then incorporated into new designs. Illustrated books of designs such as Owen Jones' *Grammar of Ornament* (1856) influenced ceramic design. The avant-garde designer Christopher Dresser, who published his *Principles of Decorative Ornament* in 1873, put many of his ideas into practice. His use of angular forms broke away from more conventional pottery shapes. Between 1879 and 1882 he was involved with the Linthorpe Art

Pottery in Middlesbrough. The flask (29), inspired by Peruvian pottery, was produced there following his designs. Other potters, such as the independently-working Martin brothers, also reflected this diverse interest in their work. Their saltglazed stoneware (30) drew on Nature as well as medieval and Japanese styles for inspiration.

30 *Stoneware vases*
English, Martin brothers, Southall,
(left to right)
1905, 1902, 1903, 1902

Experimental Techniques

*31 Earthenware vase and cover
English, Ruskin Pottery, West
Smethwick, 1906-09
32 Earthenware vase
English, Pilkington's Tile & Pottery
Company, about 1907*

Art-Directors, designers and chemists played a prominent role in early-20th-century pottery-making. They aimed to achieve a harmony between form and decoration. Potters like William Howson Taylor were especially interested in the glaze effects of oriental ceramics. Howson Taylor established a pottery in Birmingham in 1898, later known as the Ruskin Pottery, named after the critic John Ruskin. He spent years perfecting his unique 'soufflé' and 'flambé' glazes. The covered vase (31) shows the dramatic effect of a mottled green flambé glaze.

Experimental glazes, such as crystalline and

31

opalescent, were also produced by Pilkington's Tile & Pottery Company near Manchester, established in 1891. The company frequently collaborated with distinguished designers such as Walter Crane and C.F.A. Voysey. From about 1906, Pilkington's introduced lustre painting. This lustred vase (32), with fish decoration, was painted by Richard Joyce, who worked at Pilkington's between 1903 and 1931. Joyce was particularly adept at capturing the movement of animals and fish in his work.

Other artists and sculptors worked more independently. Phoebe Stabler, who trained at the

32

33 *Earthenware figure
'Lavender Woman'
English, Phoebe Stabler, 1911*

34 *Stoneware bowl
English, Reginald F. Wells,
about 1925*

Liverpool Art School between 1901 and 1904, worked in a variety of media including pottery. She produced small ceramic sculptures such as *Lavender Woman* (33), made in 1911. Later she worked for the Poole Pottery in Dorset where some of her sculptures, including *Lavender Woman*, were put into factory production.

Reginald F. Wells, also a trained sculptor, was one of the earliest of the 20th-century independent studio potters. He set up a studio in Kent, moving to London in 1909 and then to Sussex in 1925. Like other early studio potters he was greatly influenced by English slipwares and oriental stonewares. This footed bowl (34), glazed in white with green copper flashes, follows in the Eastern tradition.

The Studio Potter

Bernard Leach (1897-1979) set up the St Ives Pottery, Cornwall, in 1920, on his return from Japan where he had first learnt to make pottery. Leach's influence was far-reaching, particularly through his writings like *A Potter's Book*, published in 1940. Despite the activities of earlier potters like the Martin brothers and Reginald Wells, he is often considered to be the 'originator' of the studio pottery movement in Britain. Leach and Shoji Hamada (1894-1978), who came over from Japan, were inspired by earlier forms including English slipware and oriental stonewares. They sought to revive the traditional skills of the potter – preparing the clay and glaze, making the pots and firing the kiln. The large dish (35), made in 1926, shows Leach's use of

35 *Slipware dish*
English, Bernard Leach,
St Ives, 1926

the European slipware technique, whereas Shoji Hamada's vase (36) looks to the East for inspiration. The 'Leach tradition', as it is sometimes known, was not just about pottery-making, but also about a way of life, embracing both ethical and spiritual values.

In the 1930s, potters like Staite Murray (1881-1962) and his pupil Sam Haile (1909-1948) were influenced by new developments in contemporary art. Staite Murray viewed himself as an artist not a potter and Sam Haile produced some of the most inventive and

36

37

challenging of pre-war pottery. Like Staite Murray, Haile exhibited in fine art galleries, giving his pots titles like paintings. The thrown stoneware vase, entitled *Swan Song* (37), shows his interest in the relationship between surface and form, painting and pottery.

The post-war years have seen a broadening of the range of studio pottery and a blurring of the boundaries between art and craft. Some potters have followed in the 'Leach tradition', others have worked in a more experimental way. Lucie Rie (1902-1995) is regarded as one of the most important post-war studio potters. Born in Austria, Rie settled in England as a refugee and for fifty years experimented with form, colour and texture, mainly concentrating on thrown bowls and vases. The vase (38), with flared rim, has been thrown in a stoneware stained with colours in order to create a spiralled effect.

Pottery-making is a living craft and studio potters continue to produce a vast variety of ware, satisfying both practical needs and aesthetic ones.

36 *Stoneware vase with tenmoku glaze*
Shoji Hamada, St Ives, about 1935
37 *Stoneware vase*
'Swan Song'
English, T.S. 'Sam' Haile, 1938
38 *Stoneware vase*
English, Lucie Rie, 1980

Suggested Reading

Paul Atterbury (Ed.), *The Parian Phenomenon*,
Richard Dennis, 1989

Victoria Bergesen, *Encyclopaedia of British Art Pottery*,
Barrie & Jenkins, 1991

Victoria Bergesen, *Majolica*,
Barrie & Jenkins, 1989

E. Myra Brown and Terence A. Lockett (Eds.), *Made in Liverpool - Liverpool Pottery and Porcelain 1700-1850*,
National Museums & Galleries on Merseyside, 1993

Alan Caiger-Smith, *Tin-Glaze Pottery*,
Faber & Faber, 1973

Ronald G. Cooper, *English Slipware Dishes*,
Alec Tiranti, 1968

John and Margaret Cushion, *A Collector's History of British Porcelain*
Antique Collectors' Club, 1994

Diana Edwards, *Black Basalt*,
Antique Collectors' Club, 1994

F.H. Garner and Michael Archer, *English Delftware*,
Faber & Faber, 1972 (Revised edition)

Geoffrey Godden, *Godden's Guide to European Porcelain*,
Barrie & Jenkins, 1993

Griselda Lewis, *A Collector's History of English Pottery*,
Antique Collectors' Club, 1985

Adrian Oswald, R.J.C. Hildyard and R.G. Hughes, *English Brown Stoneware 1670-1900*,
Faber & Faber, 1982

Bernard Rackham, *Medieval English Pottery*,
Faber & Faber, 1972 (Revised edition)

R. Reilly, *Wedgwood*, 2 volumes
Macmillan, 1989

Paul Rice and Christopher Gowing, *British Studio Ceramics*,
Barrie & Jenkins, 1989

Alan Smith, *Liverpool Herculaneum Pottery*,
Barrie & Jenkins, 1970